W9-AXH-715

OCEAN LIFE UP CLOSE

Sea Urchins

by Heather Adamson

BELLWETHER MEDIA • MINNEAPOLIS, MN

Note to Librarians, Teachers, and Parents:

Blastoff! Readers are carefully developed by literacy experts and combine standards-based content with developmentally appropriate text.

Level 1 provides the most support through repetition of high-frequency words, light text, predictable sentence patterns, and strong visual support.

Level 2 offers early readers a bit more challenge through varied simple sentences, increased text load, and less repetition of high-frequency words.

Level 3 advances early-fluent readers toward fluency through increased text and concept load, less reliance on visuals, longer sentences, and more literary language.

Level 4 builds reading stamina by providing more text per page, increased use of punctuation, greater variation in sentence patterns, and increasingly challenging vocabulary.

Level 5 encourages children to move from "learning to read" to "reading to learn" by providing even more text, varied writing styles, and less familiar topics.

Whichever book is right for your reader, Blastoff! Readers are the perfect books to build confidence and encourage a love of reading that will last a lifetime!

This edition first published in 2018 by Bellwether Media, Inc.

No part of this publication may be reproduced in whole or in part without written permission of the publisher. For information regarding permission, write to Bellwether Media, Inc., Attention: Permissions Department, 5357 Penn Avenue South, Minneapolis, MN 55419.

Library of Congress Cataloging-in-Publication Data

Names: Adamson, Heather, 1974- author.
Title: Sea urchins / by Heather Adamson.
Description: Minneapolis, MN : Bellwether Media, 2018. | Series: Blastoff! Readers. Ocean life up close | Audience: Age 5-8. | Audience: Grades K to grade 3. | Includes bibliographical references and index. | Description based on print version record and CIP data provided by publisher; resource not viewed.
Identifiers: LCCN 2016059015 (print) | LCCN 2017017259 (ebook) | ISBN 9781626176461 (hardcover : alk. paper) | ISBN 9781681033761 (ebook)
Subjects: LCSH: Sea urchins–Juvenile literature.
Classification: LCC QL384.E2 (ebook) | LCC QL384.E2 A165 2018 (print) | DDC 593.9/5–dc23
LC record available at https://lccn.loc.gov/2016059015

Editor: Nathan Sommer   Designer: Lois Stanfield

Printed in the United States of America, North Mankato, MN.

Table of Contents

What Are Sea Urchins?

purple
sea urchin

Sea urchins look like tiny fireworks under the sea. These **echinoderms** are known for their spiky **spines**.

Other Echinoderms

sand dollars

sea cucumbers

sea stars

red sea urchin

They move, eat, and live on the ocean floor. There are more than 800 types of sea urchins.

Sea urchins are found along ocean floors around the world. They live in **coral reefs**, kelp forests, and rock pools.

Sea urchins do not swim. They move along the bottom of the ocean using tiny **tube feet**.

Species Spotlight
PURPLE SEA URCHIN

life span:
up to 50 years

depth range:
0 to 525 feet
(0 to 160 meters)

purple sea urchin range =

N
W • E
S

conservation status: **least concern**

Extinct	Extinct in the Wild	Critically Endangered	Endangered	Vulnerable	Near Threatened	Least Concern

Spiky, Spiny Bodies

Sea urchins are small and round.
The smallest ones are less than
0.5 inches (1.3 centimeters) across!

The largest can be 7 inches (19 centimeters) across. Many are about the size of a tennis ball.

Sea Urchin Sizes

Smallest

Echinocyamus scaber

actual size

0.2 inches
(0.6 centimeters)

Largest

red sea urchin

average human

7 inches
(19 centimeters)

Sea urchins come in many different colors. They range from blue to light pink!

flower urchin

Their spines can be sharp or **wispy**. Some sea urchin spines are **venomous**.

Identify a Sea Urchin

spines

tube feet

mouth

A hard shell covers the soft bodies of some sea urchins. All sea urchins have a mouth near the bottom of their bodies.

They have five teeth. The teeth can grow back if they fall out!

teeth

Algae Eaters

Sea urchins are hungry creatures. They spend most of their time eating or resting.

black
sea urchin

Their tube feet move them around as they eat. The feet also help push food to their mouths.

Catch of the Day

algae

common mussels

kelp

Algae is a favorite meal for sea urchins. They use their teeth to **scrape** it off rocks and coral.

These **omnivores** also eat mussels, barnacles, and dead fish.

barnacles

Sea Urchin Life

Sea urchins have many **predators**. They are a favorite meal for hungry crabs, eels, and sea otters.

Some use their venomous spines for protection.

wolf eel

Sea Enemies

California sheepheads

sea otters

wolf eels

sea otter

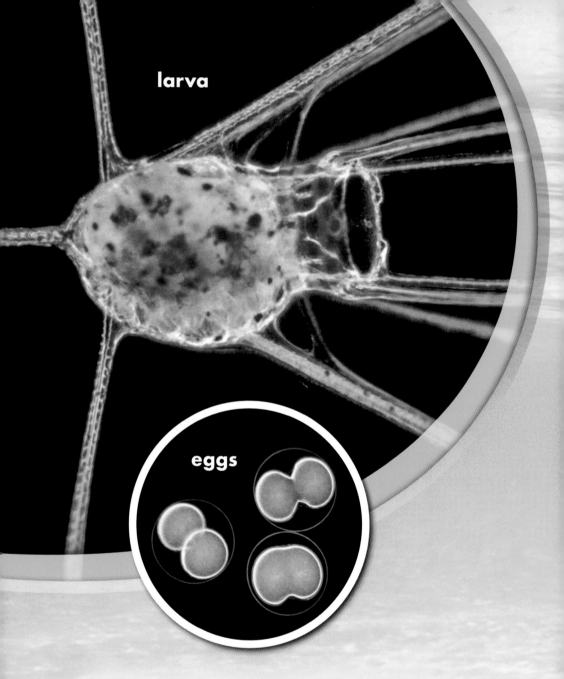

larva

eggs

Sea urchins start life as tiny
eggs floating in the water. The
eggs become tiny **larvae**.

The larvae grab onto rocks or pieces of coral. Soon, they will grow to become adult sea urchins!

slate pencil urchin

Glossary

algae—plants and plantlike living things; most kinds of algae grow in water.

coral reefs—structures made of coral that usually grow in shallow seawater

echinoderms—members of a group of ocean animals that pump water instead of blood; sea stars and sea urchins are echinoderms.

larvae—early, tiny forms of an animal that must go through a big change to become adults

omnivores—animals that eat both plants and animals

predators—animals that hunt other animals for food

scrape—to rub something sharp against a surface

spines—sharp body parts that cover sea urchins

tube feet—leg-like tubes that help sea urchins move around and hold food

venomous—able to produce venom; venom is a poison sea urchins make.

wispy—something that looks and feels fine and feathery

To Learn More

AT THE LIBRARY

Magby, Meryl. *Sea Urchins*. New York, N.Y.:
PowerKids Press, 2013.

Pettiford, Rebecca. *Sea Stars*. Minneapolis, Minn.:
Bellwether Media, 2017.

Rajczak, Michael. *Sea Urchins*. New York, N.Y.:
Gareth Stevens Publishing, 2016.

ON THE WEB

Learning more about sea urchins
is as easy as 1, 2, 3.

1. Go to www.factsurfer.com.

2. Enter "sea urchins" into the search box.

3. Click the "Surf" button and you will see a
   list of related web sites.

With factsurfer.com, finding more
information is just a click away.

Index